The Holy Worm
of Praise

The Holy Worm
of Praise

Poems

Philip Schultz

Harcourt, Inc.

NEW YORK   SAN DIEGO   LONDON

Requests for permission to make copies of any part of the work should be
mailed to the following address: Permissions Department, Harcourt, Inc.,
6277 Sea Harbor Drive, Orlando, Florida 32887-6777.

www.HarcourtBooks.com

Library of Congress Cataloging-in-Publication Data
Schultz, Philip.
The holy worm of praise: poems/Philip Schultz.—1st ed.
p.   cm.
ISBN 0-15-100666-0
I. Title.
PS3569.C5533 H6 2002
811'.54—dc21   2001003905

Text set in Ehrhardt MT
Designed by Cathy Riggs
First edition
K J I H G F E D C B A

Printed in the United States of America

For Monica

And none passes but the lonely seeker of pearls.

— WANG CHIEN

Contents

PART 3

The Holy Worm
of Praise

PART 1

The Holy Worm of Praise

to my friends on my fiftieth birthday

Let's raise our glasses and give thanks
to our great excitement and hunger
for the hereafter the joyful sleep
of expectation the Pentecostal suffering
that seizes entire winter afternoons in amber
our best days that shake us with fear and envy
our nights of provocative kissing
behind hotel rhododendrons
the secret lives we cannot remember
the deathbeds we visit like locusts
like holy scripture the fragile facade
of our psyche and its ricocheting runways
our appetite for remorse and belly-laughter and Kafka
our Knights of Infinite Resignation
our merciless opinions and monotonous disappointments
which fill our mouths with ash and feathers
our successes which beat us unconscious
demanding homage and impeccable manners
the white noise of self-loathing
and boomerang of self-pity
our kowtowing and bootlicking and toad-eating
the propitious future of our unforgiving past
our quoting Descartes without thinking
our pockets filled with blasphemy and fluster
our enemies who find us original and therefore hateful
our stuttering like Moses whom God entrusted
with so many important messages
the mistakes we mistook for privilege
the allegiance pledged to satisfaction

Change

You wake up earlier than usual,
everything feels new, irrevocable,
like the light hovering near the ceiling
in silken scarves—you can taste it
on your tongue, fizzing like dry ice,
on the tips of your fingers, salty
like ocean foam. Your shadow
is sitting on the edge of your bed,
stretching. It has already brushed its teeth
and shaved but usually you rise together
with the light (which is now hovering near the window)
—wasn't it once amber or outsized, like a splinter?
Surely you've never tasted it before: lavender,
like lilacs on the first fine day of May,
the happiest of seasons. Now your heart
is thumping like a tail—perhaps you've grown
something inside you, a shinbone or webbing
between your toes? But nothing feels late
or newly arrived, nothing is absent,
like a cramp or favorite flavor,
nothing feels grievous or disquieting,
burdensome or flagrant or atrocious,
you don't feel greedy or lusty (no more than usual),
your fingers and toes wiggle and the hair in both ears
remains calm and the hair on your chest is drifting peacefully.
But something is different,
refined like an eyebrow dormer, enhanced
like a slap on the back at the right moment,
a smile thirty years late and therefore all the sweeter....
Yes, something is rising in your body like a tide
of forgiveness or a breath at long last released,

a kind of slow waltzing in the mind's fiery sky
where every cloud suddenly stands and leaves the table
when only a moment ago the din of conversation
and clinking glasses was deafening and now you are alone
with the music of your most somber breathing—yes,
something has changed that has changed everything else,
has overtaken you like a memory of the future
that appears at your side winking as if to suggest
a new arrangement, as in a novel of manners
where everyone suddenly changes partners
and is dancing with someone they love so profoundly
clocks all over town begin chiming so loudly
you cannot hear what you are whispering over
and over again like a chant which echoes
like a heartbeat on your tongue—Monica Monica Monica . . .

A Woman's Touch

The keen shadowy
unwavering elegance of
the unexpected, unsuspecting grace of
the perfect shell of   not nature exactly
but   the comforting heft of
say, a heart of palm   a salt lick
a sculptured lip   a kiss   a

woman's   light
the   ephemera
the sheen of   hair of flesh of
eyes opening   like
windmills   vast fields of
windmills   shredding
huge inhalations of
the earth's breath   into
whispers of   affection

exploding like   halos of
light   like Beethoven   like
boisterous fingers   colliding
over ivory teeth   like cacophonous
symphonies of   raspberries
whole fields of   black pungent
juice   dripping, the tongue
the valve of   the human throat
dilated   opened full   torque
the torrid   outburst of
sound   moving out of   the body

prismatic   rainbowy
halos of   light

rippling over   vast fields of
the earth's plummeting
body   the keen shadowy
elegance of   the smooth unwavering
grace of   the great comforting
sculptured   kiss of
the ocean   breaking   inside
the mouth   yes   the touch
of her   changing   every
stone   spoon   stuttering
breath into   light   yes
light

Lord

Epithalamion

Now we shall live in each other
the way we live in weather
the way cardinals live
in our backyard all winter
climbing the sky's staircase
one stuttering step at a time
the way snow drifts outside
our window in endless folds
the way the wind complains
to the maples and sycamores
and carries their seed
from season to season
the way rain whispers your name
just before dawn shakes off its last shadow
the way we live in our story
without doors or windows
without question

Courtship According to My Guardian Angel Stein

Tradition demands that the hand you kiss
shouldn't tighten into a fist, but never try to
make nice when she's washing venetian blinds
or talk about old loves when she's drinking wine.
Schopenhauer said a woman by nature is meant to obey
but he also wrote at great length about suicide
and don't even think about removing her nightgown
after her mother phones. A pretty face doesn't make
for a good wife, a crooked foot is better than a crooked mind
and everyone knows courtship begins after marriage
and continues into death and if it seems you can do
nothing right it may be what she likes about you most.
If she says no one will love you half as much tell her
half a story is a story nonetheless. After the wedding
it's too late for regrets and everything ends with weeping.
In other words: Man thinks and God laughs and shrouds
are made without pockets. Be grateful for a home.

Flying Dogs

In early spring color pokes its chilly nose through the earth
reminiscing about past hibernations with ocean winds
inflating the sky one billowing cloud at a time and trees shed
metaphysical shadows that drift lazily along the river
known for its sexual boasting while brownstones rub
against tenements like cats unfurling in windows—
but it's the dogs who are flying! Gus, our smooth Fox Terrier,
rises on white and brown spotted wings while Benya, our black Lab mix,
loop-the-loops on powerful hawk wings, both gliding over rooftops
scaring up flocks of pigeons as neighbors climb onto fire escapes
to watch them nosedive and whirl high over Charles Street. Dylan
the cross-eyed Dalmatian is up there with Betsy the Saluki and Ruggles
the Chow Chow, who smells like Quasimodo, is double-dipping Matty
the ballbrain Irish Setter who'd go to Mars to fetch, and there's Hector
the submissive Whippet and his girlfriend, Tulip, the pertinacious Pekinese,
whooping it up with Sir Quintin the operatic Golden who's howling
something Verdi high over Sheridan Square. Yes, it's spectacular:
Giant Schnauzers, somersaulting Newfoundlands and Portuguese Water Dogs
bounding over Great Pyrenees, who can boogie-woogie with the best,
Bearded Collies, benighted Dobermans and happy-go-lucky Akitas,
forlorn Bull-mastiffs, beset Rhodesians, bandy Malamutes and Pharaoh Hounds
flying around water towers high over celebratory bridges stretching from one
surprising moment to another in this city where I lived deep in winter long
before I met you or imagined a smile so beguiling light would thaw
and the horizon vibrate like a violin string.

City Dogs

      Just
this New York morning
they're everywhere, in parks,
running with the runners
around reservoirs, up and down
windy canyons river streets,
trotting with rollerbladers and flipping
with the frisbees and Great Lawn acrobats—
nostrils pumping, ear flaps erect and eyes
rolled back, endlessly sniffing out
the metaphysical possibilities
in the simple walk after dinner
where every tree is an investigation
of the sublime, nothing foul enough
to satisfy their instinct for heresy—
aloof, bemused and ecstatically enthusiastic
mixes of every imaginable kind, fancy over-
fluffed pedigrees prattling toward pedicures,
Saturday afternoon perambulations in Village runs,
or Sunday morning powwows in Central Park, where,
let's face it, you see ordinary hounds so overtrained
in culinary arts they're epicures of the ethereal,
aestheticians and fungivorous purveyors of
every municipal mile of corroding scent—yes!
they love to feel the city on their paws,
that pulsing beat and architectonic whines
and salutations, hellos and good-byes,
the subway's plaintive eulogy
to all that's passed and forgotten
so deep beneath our refined relapses,
not to mention, cacophonous

rattling transformations of subterranean desire,
the recessive circles of time, no, yes,
these munificent beings are never imprisoned by ideals,
never molested by subterfuge or blindsided
by impious dreams of grandeur,
instead, they feel their lives vibrate
through their limbs like sonic booms,
constantly inhaling truck-and-bus-and-car fumes
like true citizens of the upper underground, peripatetic
city-dwelling native American sophists nonpareil
they have, so to speak, their noses to the ground,
while we, napkin-users of somewhat discreet inclinations,
with all our inelegant acquisitions, trot happily behind—oh
how I envy them their recherché snouts and self-obsessed tails
counting millimeters of delight, sniffing at every
passing crotch with nothing to lose
but another slice of humble pie; here, once again,
I'm following a mixed breed named Benya and
a relentlessly energetic smooth Fox Terrier named Gus
through every deadly sin and various bad humors,
stretched and yanked against all the unnatural restraints of . . .
call it civilization or the light at the end of the millennium
that is this great jungle gym of overreaching
we've somehow imprisoned ourselves within—this city life,
this maze, this unannealing shout and unfurling spray
of indignity in which each moment is an opportunity
for celebration wherein our tolerance for ecstasy
is tested hourly and apparently only dogs behave
with proper humanity so let's bow our heads
and honor every living thing
Amen!

Marking

Gus and Benya are busy this early morning,
sniffing out scents other dogs
left maybe late last night or
years ago. When they find
something interesting
they lift their rear right leg
and close their eyes and piss
with great deliberation.
But then who doesn't
like to have
the last word.

On First Hearing of Your Conception

Premature no doubt, my heading north
through the kitchen to the dining room
which is south but also west depending on
whether one is going forward to the future
or backward toward the middle of what
used to be my life in the shadows of the
living room which is now a place you will
pass through on your way to grander things.
Indeed, one must ponder the importance of
this autumn light which seems more robust
in each window. Yes, I'm walking in circles
while your mother reads about the drama
of evolution which took its time building
toward its denouement from amoebae to
somersaulting the hectic surf of our most
epic journey. Weigh each drip of gravity,
lift the tiny idea of your arms, defy the odds,
evolve.

PART 2

The Monologue

I lived in a monologue a long time.
It rambled on about people it impressed,
work it had done, prizes it had won.
It remembered every insult. Agreed
with no one. Mourned the living
and sanctified the dead. Insisted
it knew what was best for me.
Whispered in my ear like a lover
who didn't know my name.
The past was its domain.
Forgive no one, it said. Abstain.
Inherit the kingdom of death.

Disintegration

the way the mind leaves fingerprints on   every memory tissue
say: all those dreams auditioning for   infinitesimally minor roles   in

insignificant family dramas   walking thin lines   between abstract design
and routine delusion   not being whole   but disavowed   as in: denuded,

it happens so quickly   one minute your ideas are listening   and then pain
explodes into chronic babble   slicing the tongue into fervent   opinions,

suddenly everything is: twitching   the left side of your body   is: laughing,
but you feel   nothing   while the body is hysturicall   wit juy   forget ieet,

play it no hind, relux,   there are mulch mare spectickulair   events lappening
hang loose Mr. Moose   dear sweetcaboose   I'm stuck up ta me noose in rust

compost   lust und deluge   onelittlepiggietwoolittlepiggie   eee ful
like ragin urge   cause ieet huurts   it's allyacando   deer Gid

is: scream me fuckin heedoff   furst thun in da mournin   duurrlin

The Inside and The Outside

The outside is bigger,
especially at night
when you turn the lights on,
there it is,
surrounding everything,
not worrying.
This drives the inside crazy,
makes it want to go further inside
until it has become its own outside
until it expects nothing.
It likes to stand at its window
looking at the outside
being so pleased with itself,
with what it has evolved into
without any help from anyone,
not even those of us who go
from one to the other
not knowing exactly
where we are.

The Nutritive Values

Sometimes we just turn and say something
and our words surprise us. Then we wake up
in the middle of a thought wondering why
we decided to disown entire periods
of our existence. To live backwards.
It never really makes any difference
what we say exactly. Disappointment
is diving from a great height into
an empty idea. Not the actual pain
but staring into the mirror knowing
we're what's missing. Consider
the circumstances: once we were children,
smaller persons, who inspected shadows,
peeled every memory. Yes, people do things
to one another, usually without mercy.
They carry ideas like too many groceries.
God isn't the issue. Please stop smiling.
Consider the odds against doing anything
important. Shut the window. Swallow.
Refrain from speaking. Yes, we've done
hurtful things to good people, good things
to painful people. Remain seated until
every regret has left the auditorium.
Consider kindness. The prayerful peace
of self-forgiveness. Consider forgiveness.
Now shut your eyes and sleep. Deeply.

The Answering Machine

They don't counterfeit enthusiasm by raising their volume
or use static to suggest disdain or indignation. They don't
hold grudges and aren't judgmental. They're never too busy
or bored or self-absorbed. They possess a tolerance for isolation
and conscience and always remember who's calling. Cowardice
is permitted, if enunciated clearly. I broke off with Betsy by
telling her machine I couldn't go rafting with her in Colorado.
I meant *anywhere* and it understood perfectly. They appreciate
how much intimacy we can bear on a daily basis. When one becomes
overburdened it buries all pertinent information by overlapping.
Whatever happened, say, to Jane's sweet birthday song, hidden
under so many felicitations about my appendix operation, or Bill's
news of his father's death preempted by Helen's wedding invitation?
All these supplanted voices are a constant reminder of everything
we promised and forgot, the plaintive vowels and combative consonants
rubbing into a piercing vibrato of prayerlike insistence. Everything
we feared to say or mean; our very silence . . . an ongoing testimony
which we replay nightly and then erase to make room for more. . . .

The front left window

is where you found us every morning
little Raskolnikovs arguing brioche
and pain au chocolat, hating Sundays
and couples and bingeing on obits
and the catharsis of envy and self-pity,
lining up saltshakers next to napkin
holders like a private Stonehenge,
carrying dead ideas in bulging briefcases,
never wondering why we came here
morning after rainy morning,
unable to return to the tiny dark
of our apartments that waited
like police inspectors.

TV Series

The house is early Pittsburgh,
the furniture late Eisenhower,
reflecting a postponed refinement.
There's no basement or attic
and everyone walks about in pajamas
discussing the situation which evolves
backwards toward the future
that is omnipresent. No one prays
or suffers insomnia's narrative tension.
It's understood everyone is grateful,
at least during dinner, when expressions vary.
Cruelty is out of the question though
every ten minutes someone is insulted.
No one admits malice or is overtly profound,
yet week after week small fervid dramas dissolve
into irresolute resolutions no one remembers.
We, however, remain true believers in an ever
widening circle of fascination, while the weather
outside our picture windows grows louder
like a judgment we always secretly expected.

Ars Poetica

Here you are on a reading circuit somewhere East of Eden,
in a Comfort Inn watching *The Magnificent Seven*, again,
anticipating a roomful of Dickensians, one of whom fingers
1,000 rhyming pages on Jack the Ripper's unrequited love
for Moll Flanders' stuffed parrot, Rosy, that he'd like you
to glance at. Yesterday you drove 100 rainy miles to an Elks
convention, four furry heads bobbing on a sea of Seagrams,
two snoring before you began your crowd-warmer *Elegies
to Depression,* a third keeping time coughing while the fourth
wept uncontrollably because his horse, Polygamy, died
17 years ago that very night and you looked a little like him.
Then the Eliot experts rushed you through dinner after your plane
circled Nirvana for hours and you grabbed a leatherbound winelist
instead of your manuscript and found yourself in a church spotlight
under a swaying crucifix, staring at a list of Zinfandels with 400 feet
tapping, your sponsors wishing you'd come and gone like the women
talking of Michelangelo . . . well, soon it'll be morning and only one
Magnificent will have survived while another of the 66 people who
buy poetry books will have died and no, you don't get nosebleeds
while reading publicly, like Rilke, but, after all these years, you're still
cranking up waxed wings for one more nutsy flight, doing perhaps
what you do best, being so soulful and sensitive and all that. . . .

Juror's Manual

Today you may be called upon to judge your neighbor;
tomorrow he may be asked to judge you. Any number
of things may be implied about you. You may be kept
waiting and moved around or asked to repeat yourself
for no apparent reason. To behave as if you were superior
to your emotions or accept ideas repellent to your nature.
To reject your nature. To accept the failure of your values.
To accept a verdict so shameful your humanity is threatened.
To feel excluded, unevolved, disenfranchised, ultimately, canceled;
in other words, to surrender completely to judgment.

Three Conversations Overheard
in the Summer of 1999

1

A man yelling into a cell phone while waving at a taxi on Seventh Avenue:

She said you said I said that?
She actually said you said I said that?
Whaddya mean you don't remember exactly?

2

Two women walking down Barrow Street late at night, one says to the other:

Imagine going down this same block for eleven years
and never once noticing all these shadows.
It's like the beginning of the world, or the end.

3

A man and a woman on a beach in East Hampton, the woman says:

First a bug gets stuck in my ear.
Then we're up all night pouring olive oil into it.
Then you dream you're Bernard Malamud.
Now my grandma's dead.

On the corner

of Charles Street
Kareem the owner
of Henri Trois Antiques
yaps French Provincial
with Heidi the window
washer—a closet aesthete—
who is watching lacquered ladies
conduct a symphony
before Julio the mailman
who is leaning too far
into Mr. Danner's whiskey
breathing which is
something only Rodney
his Basset is allowed
to do while Dowen
the super is on his stoop
tapping his right foot
to all the yammering
flowing west toward
the Hudson soon,
if the wind holds,
all New Jersey will break
into communication
on this fine
first day of Spring.

Personally

I didn't fight for my country, Vietnam came and went
while I continued washing my face as if nothing happened.
What happened, exactly? All those trick questions in school
about history, me dreaming about the Warsaw Ghetto,
heroes of the French Revolution screaming freedom, equality!
The heroes in my neighborhood made doughnuts and gaskets,
felt their way around the dark without enough information.
Information is crucial, like satisfaction. But what is it, exactly?
Does anyone feel important, really? Even the big oaks we kept stabbing
—why did we hate them? They were bursting with strength and freedom,
watching us come and go like so much traffic. Every day now
something darkens, becomes less familiar, more distant. Know the feeling?
Actually, there's no feeling. Only appetite. Weather surrounding everything,
dark, wet, indifferent. I used to hide in the dirt cellar looking at Dad's boxes
of failed ideas. Like him, I take things personally, turn lights off, tighten things.
I ducked the draft, hid in fear and righteousness. The Berlin Wall went up
and came down again amid all that dust and yelling about freedom, the point is
something *happening* . . . getting a good seat at the Zeitgeist. Oaks know
equality isn't about satisfaction, but failure . . . like Dad's idea for cars to run
on Epsom salt, it didn't work but one wants to make a contribution,
be part of things, a citizen of one's sweet little slice of history. . . .

The Extra

We recognized his dark Slavic eyes
under horned helmets and sombreros,

his fervid lips behind fuming beards and putty noses.
Short, bald and bouncy, he played lunatic gangsters

with hysterical left eyes and angry pagans in Biblical epics,
but we liked him best as the hiccuping bandit in *Viva Zapata!*

and the paranoid deputy in *The Phoenix City Story*.
Doors slammed in his face without provocation

and he was never listed in the credits. Hey you, is what everyone called him.
Perhaps it was the contumacious gleam in his eye

or the congratulatory angle of his fedora,
but so many bad things happened, finally,

he just disappeared. Or retired.
Then he started showing up in our old photos,

eating oysters at Uncle Hy's first retirement party
and fixing his tie at Aunt Becky's second wedding.

Decorously ambiguous, he always kept his distance,
like a shadow. But being an extra isn't something

one just stops doing. It isn't like playing the cello.
Last week he followed me up Seventh Avenue disguised as a policeman

and this morning he stepped out of the Empire State Building
smiling like a tourist after an audience with God

and then faded into the background. Perhaps
he understands anonymity is the supreme vanity

and is trying to tell us something about forgiveness,
or begging for recognition in spectacles that end badly,

or waking into the surprising present of someone else's story.

The Stuntman

destroys his body
without mercy

understands
mercy

is out of the question
that he has nothing

to do
with ideas

or meaning
that death

is tenure
is holy

is his persona
that he must not

seek closure
or restitution

that no one notices
he's left the story

Prison Doctor

I fix every kind of stab wound, fractured clavicle,
gold teeth sliced out of sleeping mouths for trophy
earrings, all paranoia's graffiti pleading Doc please
yank this sardine-can shaft, this mea culpa, out of
my memory. I don't perform haruspical inspection,
the nasty custom, but we're all Etruscans here,
apostates suffering hallucinatory visions, exiled
from the future, fleeing God's imagination. What
Heidegger said: saying a thing brings it into being
exists here in reverse where thinking makes things
disappear: Sundays, weather, a spring afternoon
on the verandah, faith, a glimpse of infinity ... Outside
everyone is human a few hours a week, loves caveats,
explanations, identifying aspects of reality; here, time
dominates, promulgates extraordinary instincts, loves
unforgivable mistakes. I too suffer night sweats, own
curtained eyes, a persona scrubbed clean of delusion.
Sleep in a windowless room, a night screamer. Mother
was a physician, her father and grandfather all healers,
back when Main Street wasn't yet Wall Street. I came
of my own volition, believing this was the last honest place.
The truth is: I *was* already a prisoner; divided not by idea,
religion or geography, but fear of what lived in my soul's
basement. I refused to suffer the world, felt only the power
of status. Here, everyone suffers pride but status is tolerance
for despair. Honor despair, its fidelity and clarity; live beside,
before and underneath your life, let your knuckles scrape, be
a profile, a tattoo of Christ kissing himself, a leper; I say:
arrive out of Egypt, be private, all-encompassing, messy.
Fashion your own tiny acre of self, atone; live without syntax
or wings; say: no thanks. Swallow your fate. Your need to mean
something; weep an inch deeper each night. Survive thyself.

PART 3

The Dead

There are so many already. Probably
more than enough. Turn down any street
and you will see them just standing there,
waiting to be recognized. They don't mingle,
or talk. There's no news or gossip or luck.
Nothing to get used to. Or risk. Or give up.
They don't explore new neighborhoods
or notice much, preferring their own company.
They no longer have family or friends so no one
notices how little they've changed. You'll find
who you're looking for dreaming at a window,
waiting to be remembered. Anyone will do.

In Medias Res

All this is by way of saying
we found seven minutes of movie film
of a wedding, my mother's second
cousin, Henrietta's, we think,
which was taken forty years ago,
judging by my mother's age,
but imagine our surprise
rummaging in a closet
and suddenly so many familiar
faces grimacing as things
are getting started but as yet
haven't erupted into memorable,
if curious, behavior, when a quick kiss
on the back stairs is permission
to unwind toward self-invention,
or a window suddenly offers
a denatured view of the future,
which no one ever noticed before.
Yes, it's 1956 again and father is back-
slapping and ordering everyone around
and dear Aunt Rosemarie looks so elegant
smiling at the camera years before
anyone imagined they weren't thriving,
everyone so busy performing the geometry
of haphazard gestures, every upper lip
and fermenting brow frozen between
expectation and disappointment,
between wanting a little less
insulation and not feeling quite
so cheated, yes, all these names
and faces listening to their own

footsteps approaching everything
they meant to accomplish
but paused in the middle of . . .
seven minutes in a January evening
in the midst of a century still
too young to owe anyone even
one small moment of forgiveness.

The Displaced

Grandma hated the Russians who attacked the Ukrainians
who tormented the Romanians who pissed on everyone's roses
and played around with everyone's wives. This was Rochester, NY,
in the fifties, when all the Displaced Persons moved in and suddenly
even the oaks looked defeated. Grandma believed they came here
so we all could suffer, that soon we'd all dress like undertakers
and march around whispering to the dead. Mr. Schwartzman hired me
to write letters nobody answered. He wrote about Mrs. Tillem's
boardinghouse, where everyone stank of sardines and spat in the sink;
about his job at the A&P providing for everyone else's appetite.
He never wrote about what'd happened to his music or family.
Saturday mornings for two years he spoke Yiddish as I wrote
my twelve-year-old English until I found him hanging in his closet
with a note pinned to his tie: "Live outwardly, objectify!" Yes, Goethe,
famous for beating hexameters on his mistress's back while lovemaking
because art was long, life was short and the dead also didn't belong anyplace.

The Children's Memorial at Yad Vashem

For HANA AMICHAI

Inside a domed room photos of children's faces
turn in a candlelit dark as recorded voices
recite their names, ages and nationality.
"Ah, such beautiful faces," a woman sighs.
Yes, but faces without the prestige
of the future or the tolerance of the past.
Not one asks: Why is this happening to me?
They stare at the camera as if it were a commandment:
thou shall not bear false witness. . . .

Why would anyone want to take their photo,
remember what they no longer looked like?
There's no delusion in their eyes,
no recognition or longing, only
the flatness of hours without minutes,
hunger without appetite.

They understand they are no longer children,
that death is redundant, and mundane.
Expected, like a long-awaited guest
who arrives bearing the gift
of greater anticipation. Their eyes
are heavy—fear perhaps,
or the unforgiving weight
of knowledge.

Did they understand why they were so hated?
Wonder why they were Jews?

Did God hear their prayers and write
something in one of his glistening books?

Were they of too little consequence?
What did they think of God, finally?

Dante cannot help us.
Imagination is the first child in line.
They cannot help us.
It is wrong to ask them.
Philosophy cannot help us,
nor wisdom, or time.
Or memory.

We look at their faces and their faces look at us.
They know we are pious.
They know we grieve.
But they also know we will soon leave.
We are not their mothers and fathers,
who also could not save them.

I Remember

For YEHUDA AMICHAI

I remember walking you home so you could walk me home
so I could walk you halfway back, until, finally,
you walked one block to finish a last story like a blessing.

I remember our wandering around the Circus Maximus
of Times Square to Mozart, you proved, beating time
on my back, your hand in the crowd conducting ecstasy.

I remember the warm yogurt of the Dead Sea,
wiggling our toes and balancing the sun on our noses
like comedian seals, God, for once, speechless.

I remember the Jerusalem you showed me like a wound,
every tree, street, and shadowed doorway.
I remember the stars burning in the night like graves.

I remember our driving eight hundred miles
to move my mother into a nursing home, your kissing
her hand like a soldier saluting an act of courage.

I remember our silence at the Western Wall,
our prayers hovering in the air like hummingbirds.
I remember your smiling as if everything had been forgiven.

I remember our singing Vallejo, Tranströmer, Szymborska,
in a classroom, the joy in your hooded eyes,
the cancer scraping your blood like a scythe.

I remember your drifting off in cafés like an astronaut
turning in space, attached only by an umbilicus of faith,
the light in your eyes moving farther and farther away.

Alzheimer's

In the beginning it visits your mother
like a polite somewhat obtrusive stranger

whose silence, like the dripping from every faucet,
pots cracking on burners, toast abandoned like words in mid-sentence,

is vaguely disturbing,
then it's there every time you visit

in the blinking and shivering nods,
in the way her fork freezes in midair

inches and entire years from her mouth,
in the lizard's lash of her tongue removing invisible crumbs.

One day it begins answering all your questions,
insisting you are her mother father brother,

smiling like a stranger as you sit with her
upon a sofa discussing the world

she has peeled away leaf by stunned leaf
as cloud shadows cross her still bright smile

one neighborhood and street and porch at a time,
her fingers clicking on the table

as if in answer to someone's knocking.
No one is at the door of course

but you want someone to be there
just once, knocking.

Apartment Sale

Mrs. Apple thought I wasn't looking
when she dropped my mother's gold pin
down her blouse, then snorted
after haggling me to fifteen dollars
for the cherrywood breakfront
that looked exactly like the one
Jackie Kennedy had in the White House.
Mr. Pepps decided against my father's
first get-rich scheme—a flintless lighter—
but paid fifty cents for a honeymoon mug
my mother got in Atlantic City. He himself
didn't care for marriage, but liked coffee.
My mother's best friend, Bea, got
the mother-of-pearl hairbrush she coveted,
but looked insulted. The Salvation Army
took the blue sofa with a big moon stain
rising over twenty-one ocean waves.
I kept a photo of my mother standing
at attention in front of our old house,
smiling with her eyes closed, as if
she didn't want to see everything
that was going to happen. A big bow,
pink, I imagine, in her blond curls.

Nomads

I've come to clean my mother's room out,
fit everything she owned into one handbag.
"They pick things up in one room and drop
them in another," Lisa, the head nurse, says,
explaining why my mother's wedding ring
is missing. "Dementia makes them roam,
they forget which room is theirs." I look at
a photo by my mother's bedside. "You were
a beautiful child and Lill's so young and pretty.
She'd stare at it for hours. . . ." The boy looks
like me when I was three but my mother
was never slender like this woman. I wonder,
though, if she ever saw a photo of me in another
woman's room and thought I looked familiar.
I was the one thing she did right, she told me,
yet I wasn't part of the past she remembered.
"Will anyone miss this?" I ask, dropping
the photo in her bag. "No," Lisa smiles,
"nobody here misses anything."

Stories

LILLIAN SCHULTZ, 1907–1998

Nights she counted coins from my father's vending machines,
stacked nickels dimes pennies into houses, neighborhoods
with streets and backyards and little boys under kitchen tables
watching their mother's feet tapping, her nails on waxy wood
splaacckkcctt splaacckkcctt until her eyes got sleepy and she
picked me up and carried me to the tub, water jumping
raauuummppphh and slid me down the steaming, her breasts
wet and soapy as she scrubbed me a plump pink chicken,
humming *lala aaa uuiieeoo laaa* and lifted me high and kissed me,
singing, My darling little man! and carried me to my room
to dry me in a big soft towel while I pretended not to like it,
twisting as she rubbed harder. Ticklish, eh! she laughed, ticklish
little rabbit, her fingers crinkly with talcum, jumping on my stomach
until I howled—Oh, I could eat you up *arruummpphh!* munching
my fingers toes, my heart kaalluummpping as she told stories
about being a girl when every yard had gardens like countries
in Europe with cherry and black plum and apple and pear trees,
her hair so long her mother braided it in pink ribbons and all
the women wore kerchiefs and bright peasant dresses waving
like flags up one street and down another smiling good morning
telling every brilliant thing their children did with one hand tied
behind their backs and all the old widows deep in windows, window
widows she called them, always complaining but everyone spoke
five languages at once and every house was white with red shutters
and she and her sister walked around flirting with boys in derbies
and every spring Saturday she helped her mother do wash in the backyard
and the splashing soaked the air and the grass glistened and everywhere
in branches cardinals and blue jays and robins singing and in winter

the snow came blowing off the lake like clouds burying the houses
and men tied colored hankies to car antennas but children switched them
so every morning the cursing and now she was laughing, her head back
as I moved closer and she put her arms around me and rocked us
and I wanted it to last forever, the two of us, together, always.

Darwin, Sweeping

It's not light yet and Dowen is out sweeping our tenement steps,
the same ones he used to paint every few months. Somehow
the color was never right. A super for forty years, everyone
on the block knows him but can't get his name right—Hey, Darwin
come fix my flood, I've been burgled, my husband beat me again,
I'm afraid of the dark. Once a girlfriend left me twice in one week
and he understood. I didn't, but he did. Hey, Darwin, is the Mayor coming?
I smile and he smiles back. Bernice, his wife of fifty-one years, died last week
and that's why he's sweeping the steps, the walk, the street too. Once
he painted our steps a shy jellyfish red, the kind you see off the islands
of the Galápagos Archipelago and overnight our building was an island
unto itself, a glimpse of infinity, a moment of discovery
on a long voyage home, part of the overall picture.

The Eight-Mile Bike Ride

In memory of JOHN CHEEVER

Sundays we cranked old bikes up hills
until our legs burned and our faces glowed
and our breath twisted down winter inroads
and wind froze our hands as trees measured
the glide of seasons. Splendid was his word
for that rich winding Hudson Valley country,
the hills' swaggering color, gravel sparkling,
rain on our smiling faces, the bridge slick
with first snow, each hill a challenge of chains
whish whish the sibilance of macadam—Geronimo!
he'd yell, as we'd go headlong, hands like sails.
Once he somersaulted over handlebars and gashed
his head leaving a looping red trail eight miles long
we spotted months later. But nothing mattered,
not pain which was familiar, a kind of knowing,
like skies opening deeper into light, only trees
and weather and hills mattered, as we drifted reckless
in surrender. No one told a better story. Even
the trees listened, bending to that pure Yankee
hone of language flowing like the spicy stink
of river. The air cracked as we rode around
seasons, as in his story of the swimmer,
the light beginning in summer, fierce and dark
in windows, all those lives hurrying toward
an end which is always surprising, even
when expected. Once we stopped to watch
the night rinse through the heavens, the stars
so silent he said they looked lonely. I think

he meant to tell me that all good stories
are sad, finally, and we make such good stories,
but the window lights grow brighter, burning
with all the others as they do now in memory,
where we are splendid still, every Sunday.

The Silence

for R J

You always called late and drunk,
your voice luxurious with pain,
I, tightly wrapped in dreaming,
listening as if to a ghost.

Tonight a friend called to say your body
was found in your apartment, where
it had lain for days. You'd lost your job,
stopped writing, saw nobody for weeks.
Your heart, he said. Drink had destroyed you.

We met in a college town, first teaching jobs,
poems flowing from a grief we enshrined
with myth and alcohol. I envied the way
women looked at you, a bear blunt with rage,
tearing through an ever-darkening wood.

Once we traded poems like photos of women
whose beauty tested God's faith. "Read this one
about how friendship among the young can't last,
it will rip your heart out of your chest!"

Once you called to say J was leaving,
the pain stuck in your throat like a razor blade.
A woman was calling me back to bed
so I said I'd call back. But I never did.

The deep forlorn smell of moss and pine
behind your stone house, you strumming
and singing Lorca, Vallejo, De Andrade,
as if each syllable tasted of blood,
as if you had all the time in the world . . .

You knew your angels loved you
but you also knew they would leave
someone they could not save.

Mr. McGuire

Everything is downhill after you turn fifty,
he said on my forty-ninth birthday. Pigeons
also gossip, he said when Mr. Potts told him
what Mrs. Pagalucci said about his torch singing.
Everyone leads a secret life, he said the third time
I locked myself out of my apartment. We swapped
frustrations: the latest nosedive of heroics, how they
didn't sweep the street like they used to, the roof
collapsing under the weight of his eighty-eight winters.
He knew the city when it was a long hello and everyone
spit-shined their oxfords, the consonants backflipping
off his tongue like a boy into the Hudson back when
the century was so new he carried it in his pocket
like a silver dollar. I didn't think of him as old but
a widower gruff with complaining Steinbrenner
should be horsewhipped and sent back to Cleveland.
What the Yankees needed was a real New Yorker.
His egg frying set off alarms throughout the building
but there's no stink this morning. After fifty years
of his being lively on the stairs, the stairs are silent.

The Dalai Lama

for JOSEPH BRODSKY

It was a lovely spring morning in Greenwich Village
in 1981 and I was wandering about muttering to myself
about my work, a woman, the usual things, when I bumped
into him. . . . Lost in thought, eh? he laughed. Indeed. Lost
in too much "me" . . . unlike him, I never stood up to an idea
that stood up to me, said good-bye to country, family, friends,
everything. Pilgrim hero in need of a haircut, he was on his way
to see the Dalai Lama, who'd summoned him! But what does one
say to *the* Dalai Lama? he asked. I said: Joseph, be yourself,
once again speak up! Wonderful advice, he yelled, I'll do just that!
hurrying off toward his destiny, which we all know was great.
To this day I wonder what they talked about, the world
as we know it, or would like it to be, or something more mystical,
like the sadness of exile, and the courage of spring.

To William Dickey

I was his student but he treated me like a colleague,
introduced me to Mr. Berryman, and Theodore Roethke.
The last time I saw him his hair was dyed henna, his wife
was gone, he introduced me to his boyfriend and vodka

mixed with milk, insisted I read H. Crane, Dickinson, too.
Once I called after finding my house empty. M, I said,
had left me again, as he said she would; he demanded
I toss Crane and read Basho, I needed "lightness" but only

on a full stomach. Then he sang, "That evil passed, so also
may this," quoting an anonymous poet living in exile.
The day he died I dreamed I was hurrying to his house
with a new poem, yelling, Bill, I think you'll like this one.

Sitting cross-legged on a rug in his Victorian house
high above San Francisco, we spoke in Haiku, drank vodka
mixed with milk. Smiling, he asked me to read it again,
but more slowly this time, in order to taste the music.

Stein, Good-bye

What kind of guardian angel are you,
moping at the window, wings drooping
and domed brow bent as if listening to
the sad music of the spheres? Old friend,
don't be forlorn, soon you'll be busy
recycling another recalcitrant soul back
into human circulation. Isn't it satisfying
to notch a wing under restitution? I'm not
ungrateful, I'll miss the pickled herring
on your breath, the Stetson that belonged
to Wild Bill Levi, the first Jewish cowboy,
your pacing in hallways as I labored to
deliver my first sestina, your dentures
clicking on subways, a flatulent Talmudist
seized with Solomonic wisdom. It's time
to find another soul to rescue. I'm still
bewildered, tremble with fear of judgment,
suffer my rewards and believe in rejuvenation . . .
a reluctant dancer who must keep moving,
slowly, into the future. . . . Stein, good-bye.

The dark between

the starry hush
and shadowy rust
in the wallpaper's bloom

the child's sofa bed dreams
and warped room's well
in the echoing house

the collected escapes
and Biblical hymns
in the whispering weeds

the long hungry weep
and suitcase shame
in the Diaspora sprawl

the scrap metal dead
and horses of rage
down kettledrum stones

the history of black sighs
and sway of great whys
in the stained glass rain

the miraculous wounds
and steerage eyes
of the enormous dead

the doing what we must
and stars diced to ice
in the boomeranging night

the nation of bells
and extravagant return
to the God no one judged

the oblivious shrug
and traveling so far
in the dark between

Mr. Parsky

His big monkey hands slapping shiny boxes,
singing brass gold silver handles silk-lined payment plans,
an invoiced infinity with no secrets or pockets to put them in.

My father's body stripped of its nakedness,
leaking fluorescence and the stink of embalming fluid,
his mind's peeling ember still reciting Pushkin,

kicking steaming chickens into the air between swallows,
swinging freely in every direction,
his nostril antennae vibrating with a litany of insults.

Okay, Mr. Parsky, we'll take the cheapest
least shiny worm-hungry cradle-rocking
most womanly-shaped never waking one.

His eyes sprinkling the cold blue shock
of two hundred spring birds singing
open your chest and let the river out.

2

His black mule hauling a pickled gravity,
the gray sky jerked down like a shade,
expect rain he says, its sonorous riff

and cleansing scrape of robust decay
buried deep in the mind's honeycomb,
where all the guilt is stored.

He doesn't take my hand or say:
try not to understand anything
or: deplore sympathy

or: be deaf and dumb,
a troglodyte's black lichen eyes,
the sweet undertaste of the sublime,

nightmare served medium-rare
with brussels sprouts and wet crinkly spinach
lots of olive oil the expensive kind,

never says: enjoy the evolving leap
the high step of epic promise,
what he says is: hello and welcome.

3

My father's dreams—where are they?
Do they still stutter with exuberance,
pull dimes out of their ears,

believe they invented the hula hoop
but didn't get to the patent office in time,
argue with themselves in the basement all night,

squeeze greasy nickels out of candy machines,
cruise the heavens in a red Cadillac
singing *I'm a Yankee Doodle Dandy*?

4

Mr. Parsky says his boxes are made
of the kind of molecules they send to Mars,
the kind a worm bangs his head against

and piss can't rust, the kind
you can grow roots and be bottomless inside.
Seamless tugboats lugging spoiled cargoes

up and down the steaming Styx,
imagine, he says, stowaways
still dreaming of America.

5

The mess a father makes: piss-soaked sheets,
a face turning one hundred shades of blue,
choking on last words: oh it ain't gonna rain no more!

pockets full of salted IOUs,
coins from his peanut machines,
his one suit hanging in the closet like a suicide,

death no excuse not to work hundred-hour weeks,
bang hammer his way to Kingdom Come
and back each goddamn day.

Now no one's scared to step up
and slap dirt on his face, the same kind
he carried from Russia under his fingernails.

6

Mr. Parsky's rattle of mementos:
cracked dentures eyeglasses old keys,
the perfidy and hindsight he overhears,

last wishes and regrets, stone angels
bloated with Talmudic prophesy:
he is a garden of trompe l'oeils,

an implacable juggernaut,
Charon seeking verisimilitude,
his best suit pressed and pantless.

7

Mr. Parsky says: list his assets for a eulogy,
okay: a postcard of a prodigal landscape he ruminated in,
his conscience frozen like a slice of wedding cake,

a photo of his Rabbi's lugubrious eyes,
a recording of Ezekiel singing *Mack the Knife,*
the sea smell of his wife's hair in moonlight,

a fingernail clipping shaped like a bedspring,
a covetous sigh a baby tooth stained with appetite,
an arm where a boy hangs laughing upside down.

8

Mr. Parsky swings his arms around,
imagine, he says, a glittering Transcendence
hovering like a Monarch butterfly,

time's conveyor belt ticking past
like a freight car rattling the beyond,
the conductor's rouged unsmiling face nodding good-bye.

Don't ask what comes next,
the dark's an ignorant rhyme,
a spine bent into a question mark,

instead, imagine the elapsed, the gone by,
a statuesque stroll through the park,
the hunger of embryo wings.

PART 4

Souls Over Harlem

There may be always a time of innocence.
There is never a place....
—WALLACE STEVENS

1

    East
on the Long Island Expressway
toward Montauk, my wife and I
on the lam so to speak,
away
    from our appetite
for calumny, the bone scrape
and tongue-stropping angst
of the big avenues, from
the bow and genuflect
and gargoyle melancholy
of subway faces reading ads
for heraldic tattoos and Chivas swank,
the Hudson's pungent breath,
the Christmas delirium tremens—
fleeing all this on a Friday night
for a respite of two days and nights
near the ocean, in East Hampton.

2

    Seeking Mozart,
my wife tunes
to a news bulletin
declaiming here's what's happening
right *now*: a black man, one Roland J. Smith, Jr.,

alias Abubunde Mulocko, has shot
and burned eight people dead,
himself included, in Freddy's Fashion Mart,
    a clothing store
on the umbilicus of 125th Street
across from the Apollo Theater,
where he vended gold teeth,
    stolen prosthetics
and Rolex pipe dreams,
it seems this Abu-bun-de Mu-lock-o
went nuts, way over the edge
of reason, for reasons lost
as my wife finds the Jupiter
Symphony no. 40.

3

    The next morning
in our cozy kitchen
in a quiet village
near the ocean,
I read the newspaper.
    Apparently,
it happened this way:
a black record shop, a good citizen
of 125th Street for twenty years,
was being evicted by Freddy's Fashion Mart,
owned and managed by Jews
from Queens, thus months
of *burn the Jews* homonyms
while Motown and Mingus swelled bliss
over Harlem's concrete,
and Mr. Smith, alias *Mulocko,*

feeling his soul was being evicted too,
stepped into Freddy's as the chosen
messenger of the Almighty's Wrath
against the infidels.

But Freddy's rented
from a black Baptist congregation,
which owned the building
and was raising Freddy's rent,
so Freddy's raised its sublet's rent,
the black record shop—which means
Abubunde could've used a story
more open to complications
than Samson and the Philistines.

4

    Zigzagging
the hydrant spray of surf,
two brilliant canines
and one aging attendant
scouting scents left some time
before Christ discovered America,
looking perhaps
    for a spume
of illusory spice, wind
and sand speckling our faces
    under morning's
violet thumbprint, Monica,
at home making blueberry pancakes
(the kind you can taste with all
your previous lives), singing
to her flowering belly,

as our three-year-old son
    sails his ancient dreamships
off our deck into
the ocean light.

5

    The radio says:
Mulocko's conscience objected
to Vietnam—"I deny my citizenship,"
he told the Antichrist judge,
"I, my people are slaves *here,*
why should we fight your war?..."
    Another island
refugee seeking the dream
of democracy in a cardboard box,
sweeping frying polishing
to marry a doorway,
give his name to a subway grate
to earn his keep, but
    he said no, simply
refused to go, so they wrapped
him in black and white stripes,
jailed his righteous ass, so
he could think things through
for a year or two,
understand the rules,
    God's vigilante,
chained to a prison rock
in the Bronx, an immigrant
Prometheus, hammered (I imagine)
into a rusty hinge

of rage and unrequited
sorrow.

6

    I too
objected,
refused to fight
for my country, claimed
my mind was a rhapsody
of splendid stigmata opposed
to a central governing body,
pleaded argued schemed
(until they believed me)
following in the steps of my friend R
who starved himself,
spoke in hieroglyphics,
claimed he was a living stillborn,
    until, exactly
twenty-seven years ago,
he said, okay, enough
and parked on a cliff
in the cold wind of the Pacific
and stuck his mulatto face
in a plastic bag
and drank snail poison,
and burned his intestines
to an ash transparency.

7

    That was
twenty-seven years ago,
his age when

he sold everything (piano,
books, his original jazz music,
everything)
    and moved into his VW
to ponder Camus's most important question.
In grad school he was famous
for translating Celan's *Death Fugue,*
looked good in shades,
played a cool jazz piano,
his cigarette dangling
on his lower lip (a matter of principle),
    way beyond cool,
right shoulder raised
        in a turkey trot riff,
a man breathing his life in all the way
        to the last moment.
Nights we drove his VW convertible
through the wheat fields, under
the sky's lucent houseguests,
singing Yehuda Amichai
and Osip Mandelstam,
yes, he wanted to be ancient,
a Jew like me,
while I wanted a powerful black soul,
to live deep in a parenthesis,
where, like him,
    I wouldn't need anyone.

Once he said:
    he was going to lock himself up in a dead man
    he was sick of the music of human beings
Once he knocked on my door in the middle of the night
and said:
    please stay away from me

8

    Deep
in the husk of her studio
Monica pulls and twists
with acetylene flame
two-inch rods
      into faces,
half human, half beast,
heads on sticks she calls them,
cold steel transmogrified
into souls that howl deep
in our backyard under
the moon's fluorescence,
form elongated into dream
by her strong hands—
    "The Family,"
she calls them, fallen angels,
happy (I think)
to have found fertile soil
      among our maples
and sycamores and wild roses,
blooming in winter, deep
in the mind's manure—yes,
a family, no different,
finally, from any other.

9

    Tonight,
in bed, Monica remembers
her mother's argument
with memory (whether
her mother's cattle car had a stove,

she recalls something burning)—
I say, of course the mind
demands a stove, only so
much reality can be sustained
before the mind disappears
inside its dreams. I think,
of course Abubunde Mulocko
owned an argument, a stove
he couldn't forgive,
no doubt he hung out,
jived with stones,
plucked
          a few devious strings,
wore an earring in his nose ear eyebrow,
drove around his bramble-sprouting island
in an old Chevy with the top down,
watching the diaphanous stars
chariot race,
          brawled with God,
a heretical pilgrim
looking for a good-enough dream
          or legacy, or team,
to forget and forgo
his rage
and be still enough to sleep
a turtle's hermetic sleep,
maybe inch
          his way toward the other side
               of what he already knew
wasn't Paradise, just
a quiet country road (certainly
          not the Long Island Expressway

on a Friday night during rush hour),
maybe
he would've liked
to hear R's version of "Round Midnight,"
        smoke an unfiltered Lucky Strike,
stretch his unambiguous legs,
        wonder
how things might've worked out
if he'd been born only half out of luck,
        only half
the wrong shade of blue,
maybe then
he could've educated himself enough
to understand
            why
he couldn't be a citizen of *anything,*
stand straight up
            like a sycamore tree,
        be, you know, more
a part of things.

10

    My father's
immigrant eyes
flashed in the slats
of shivering rain
as he torched
a clothing warehouse
for insurance, while
I sat in the car, watching
his shadow sprinkle
a can of gasoline—poof

all six floors a blistering ladder of light
                    climbing
the sky, floating
                deep inside
the grid of my ten-year-old eyes,
the ash cloud falling
over the night—wondering

what if people are inside
what if the police come
what if mother finds out
why he wanted a witness

boomboomboom
rain hammering the hood
like fists

11

        I wake
out of a dream
of Abubunde's childhood face,
        his eyes still innocent,
tight balls of faith,
his flesh not yet peeled
apple rinds, oh
the unforgiven sins
        buried deep
in the soul's bottomless basement,
too far down to find
with a flashlight,
Monica
tucked deep
in sleep, her belly burgeoning
with our second son,

a smoky curl
    of thigh poking
out of a moment
so sweet
I watch the stars pass
deep above
this fertile island.

12

    Can
a man die
in a single English sentence?

December 15, 1972

Dear P,

*. . . R killed himself two days ago . . . he was living in his car after he sold all his
things to pay for two weeks of scream therapy after C left him and took her
daughter. . . . I saw him a week before he died . . . nothing left but pain . . . he
wanted to talk to you but you were moving around . . . he couldn't reach you . . .*

                                        K

These words bounced
all the way from San Francisco
to Provincetown . . . but I
was "moving around" . . .
ignorant of the difference
I might have made.

13

    Our son,
Eli,
loves to grab hold

and fly across
the sacred lagoon
    of the living room
in a tango
of arms feet and screams,
    invents himself
one mistake at a time.
Born on the longest day of light,
his tiny fists clenched
as if against
all that was yet to come,
his black eyes excluding no one.
Now we high step
around the house, two steps
forward, three back
and turn, do it over again,
    some nights,
when it's time to go to bed,
he points at the sky
and asks, But why?
The blackness
I think he means.
All the miles
of nothing.

14

    One day
when R was seven
his white mother
    took him aside
and said: Baby,
it hurts me to tell you

but your real daddy
was a black man.
You're only half white.
No, Daddy
isn't your father
and he doesn't
want you anymore.
Your brother and sister
can stay because
they're all white.
It's you or all of us.
It's not your fault
     but
your hair's getting curly
and your lips thick ,
You got to go
live in a foster home.
I'm so sorry,
really
I am. . . .

15

    Did Mr. Smith
suspect King Abubunde's mind
was about to go on a rampage?
That it was truth time?
    Did Mr. Smith
try to warn him not to listen
to the hundred black angels
singing in his ear?
    Some nights
R played something so fine

his quick scared eyes
became sphinxlike, dark
with a beveled-truth praise,
straight from the heart,
        and then
he'd rub his elegant hands
and laugh, Hey—
whaddya think of that, man?
        A blackbird
perched on his shoulder,
whispering
        maybe
he wasn't black *or* white
enough to survive,
        maybe
he was blurred,
like twilight.

16

        Marriage,
the daily rites
of who didn't cover
the leftovers, why the soap
isn't where it's supposed to be,
        the constant demand
of things wanting to be cooked,
cleaned, hugged and understood.
        Now
the trick is
not to think but drift
in ever-widening circles,
raking perfect camel humps

as the wind reshingles the lawn,
    and Monica
arranges lilacs, cuts, snaps
and places each flower
in window light.
    I barely recall
the man with my name
who played solitaire all night,
or what made him seem
like a stranger the morning
I left him behind
at a train station.
    Now
we have no one
but ourselves
to blame
for our happiness.

17

    "Up here
in Harlem," the president
of 125th Street Improvement District
tells the world
the next day,
    "things explode,
no one's innocent
for long."

18

    At night
Monica and I stand
in our backyard

and round
like the earth
around the sun
or is it
the other way around?
All
R ever wanted
was a proud spine,
aint like they
who got one
gonna miss a slice,
trick is
never ask
for love
while you're
on your knees.

24

Now all
anyone'll remember
is flammable paint thinner
and the semiautomatic revolver
he brandished
like a scepter,
not his royal fire
his to and fro apostolic strut
and street-corner gospels,
not his soul stitched to his face in flames;
no, they'll remember
the sacrilege up his nose
all the minstrel halos
yanked out of scorched sleeves,

they'll remember Freddy's,
the stink of human torches
burning in a discounted Hades—
    not his shadow
reciting scripture with praise,
his mind stuffed with waves
of sloshing flammable hate juice,
    not that after twenty years
on 125th Street,
            his street,
his soul drowned in diluvium waters
    because it was winter
and God
soaked his furnace
and braided his telephone wires
into a crown of fire.

25

    My wife reads
the paper's obsequy aloud,
what took place at Freddy's Fashion Mart
    two days before Christmas:
where Kareem Brunner, 23, security guard,
his best job yet, he feels up to it,
tough but kindly mien,
he'll be a success one day,
was shot and burned dead,
along with—Olga Garcia, 19,
shopping for her father and brothers
who don't like her working so hard,
    but what the hell,
this is America, man,

pull your weight
or go down Moses—
        Angeline Marrero, 20,
daughter of a Pentecostal minister,
so sweet
he named her after an angel,
        listen
she didn't know how
to open a bank account,
        imagine that,
an angel with a bank account—
        Cynthia Martinez, 19,
anxious to turn 20, so eager
not to be an American teenager—
        Garnette Ramantar, 43,
the store manager,
        fresh from Guyana,
his wife so proud
he stays up late reading
at the kitchen table, what determination,
American know-how,
she rushes to see if his car
is parked outside Freddy's,
        it is,
Sweet Jesus, oh no
not Garnette—Luz Ramos, 20,
a salesclerk, two babies,
one three, the other nine months,
        this is her first job,
look it's like this, "You get a job,
it's bad; you don't, it's bad," her brother
José tells anyone
who'll listen, "it's all crap fuck*ing* politics"—

          the moment is a tree
of hallucinations—finally
Mayra Rentas, 22,
visiting her friend Luz,
worrying about last-minute shopping,
          nothing too expensive,
she's saving for college. . . .

26

          Napoleon
the doorman
is interviewed on TV
on his way home from work,
stands on 125th Street
in front of a black hole
in the ground, shakes
his head, "Will this community
survive? Man, you
gotta be kidding."
Behind him, screams
(I imagine) ricochet
and tinsel angels
float
          in a whoosh of red air.

27

          The last entry
in R's journal reads:

          . . . *P first brought me to these cliffs the most beautiful place in the
world he said like the world was full of beauty I tried so hard to believe him I
guess I'm going to ruin it for him I always envied the dead maybe it's like the*

ocean bottomless complete unto itself not needing anything from anyone
unforgiving I wish I could forgive her the way her eyes got when she told me I
had to go away she was five years younger than I am now when she had me
once I saw her in a store and followed her as she shopped for kids' stuff
touched all those pretty clothes smiling didn't she feed me her milk didn't I
come out of her covered with her blood screaming holy jesus christ why wasn't
there any love left . . .

28

     Often
Abubunde must've wondered
what went wrong and when—
was it on a Wednesday,
Monday or snowy Friday
when his soul started to die.

     I wonder
what he did the night before
while Luz's radio sang
of innocent infatuation,
watch TV (he didn't own one),
read the Bible (he knew it by heart),
eat a last meal (no appetite),
think how his Mama,
a true believer,
made him promise
to make her proud?

29

     The ocean
lives exactly
one mile away,

churning like quicksilver,
   all that matter
constantly swirling
down
     around
and under itself,
like shadows,
while our infant son
smiles
     at the night sky
as if he understands
why
in God's name
    so many
tiny lights
seem to shimmer
a moment longer,
    without mercy,
wonder,
    or forgiveness.

Acknowledgments

THANKS TO THE editors of the following magazines in which some of the poems in this book first appeared:

Denver Quarterly: Personally; The Inside and The Outside; Disintegration

Double Take: Darwin, Sweeping

Grand Street: Souls Over Harlem (parts 10 and 16)

The Georgia Review: The Extra

The Gettysburg Review: Mr. Parsky (Part I); Flying Dogs; The Nutritive Values

The Harvard Review: The Stuntman

The Nation: The Dead; The Children's Memorial at Yad Vashem

The New Republic: Apartment Sale; I Remember

The New Yorker: The Displaced; On First Hearing of Your Conception; The Silence

The North American Review: Mr. McGuire

The Paris Review: Prison Doctor

Pequod: Mr. Parsky (complete poem)

Poetry: The Holy Worm of Praise; The dark between; The Answering Machine; The Eight-Mile Bike Ride; Change; A Woman's Touch; My Friend Is Making Himself; City Dogs; Stories; Epithalamion

The Southern Review: Mr. Parsky (parts of 1, 2 and 12 in
   different form)
Southwest Review: TV Series
The Yale Review: In Medias Res

Alzheimer's first appeared in *Sixty Years of American Poetry*
   (Academy of American Poets, Abrams).
The Answering Machine was reprinted in *New American Poets
   of the 90's,* edited by Jack Meyers & Roger Weingarten
   (Godine Publishers).
The Displaced; The Extra; In Medias Res; and The Holy
   Worm of Praise were reprinted in *Poets of the New Century,*
   edited by Rick Higgerson and Roger Weingarten (Godine
   Publishers).
My Friend Is Making Himself was reprinted in the 1997
   Anthology of Magazine Verse & Yearbook of American Poetry
   (Monitor Book Company).
The Holy Worm of Praise; Stories were reprinted in *Poetry
   Daily,* an on-line poetry anthology, May 1997 and January
   1999.
Courtship According to My Guardian Angel Stein; Stein,
   Good-bye were previously published in *My Guardian Angel
   Stein,* a chapbook (State Street Press).

I wish to thank Joseph Parisi of *Poetry* magazine, Abby Wender,
and my friends and colleagues at The Writers Studio for their
enthusiasm and faith in this book and its author.